Medieval Castle Adventure Crafts

Anna Llimós

Enslow Elementary

an imprint of

Enslow Publishers, Inc.

40 Industrial Road
Box 398
Berkeley Heights, NJ 07922
USA

http://www.enslow.com

Con

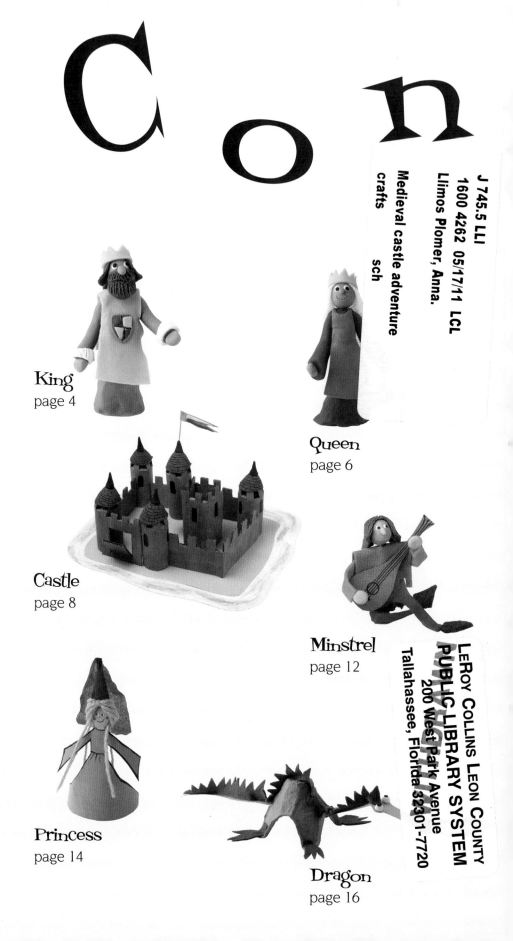
Note to Kids

The materials used in this book are suggestions. If you do not have an item, use something similar. Use any color material and paint that you wish.

You can also make up a story of your own using the crafts in this book. Put on a show for your family and friends. Use your imagination!

Safety Note

Be sure to ask for help from an adult, if needed, to complete these crafts.

tents

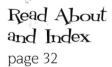

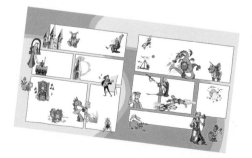

King

The king welcomes us!

6. Make the nose out of clay and attach it to the face. Flatten some clay and cut out a crown. Wrap the crown around the head.

1. Make the king's body out of clay. Make the arms out of two long pieces of clay. Attach the arms to the body with toothpicks. Wrap a piece of clay around the end of each arm for the cuffs. Use a toothpick to decorate the cuffs.

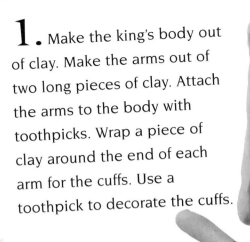

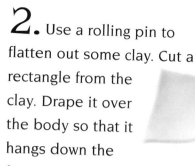

2. Use a rolling pin to flatten out some clay. Cut a rectangle from the clay. Drape it over the body so that it hangs down the front and back.

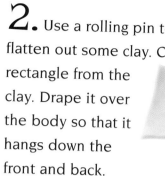

3. Make a small shield with a flat piece of clay. Decorate it as you wish.

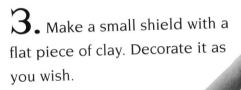

4. Use a ball of clay for the king's head and two smaller balls for the hands. Attach the head and the hands to the body with toothpicks.

5. Make the eyes out of clay and stick them onto the face. Use a rolling pin to flatten out another piece of clay. Cut out the hair and the beard. Use a toothpick to decorate the hair and beard. Stick the hair and beard onto the head.

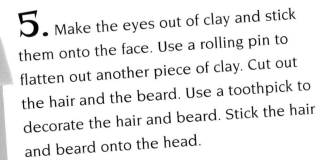

Materials

- clay
- toothpicks
- gauze
- scissors
- rolling pin
  (Ask permission first!)

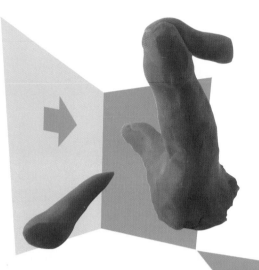

1. Make the queen's body out of clay. Make the arms out of two long pieces of clay. Attach the arms to the body with toothpicks.

2. Use a rolling pin to flatten two pieces of clay. Cut out the front and back of her dress. Place them on the body.

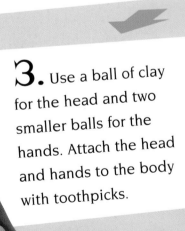

3. Use a ball of clay for the head and two smaller balls for the hands. Attach the head and hands to the body with toothpicks.

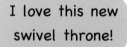

I love this new swivel throne!

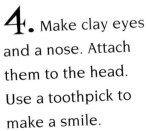

4. Make clay eyes and a nose. Attach them to the head. Use a toothpick to make a smile.

6

Queen

6. Flatten some clay and cut out a crown. Wrap the crown around the head over the veil.

5. Cut a piece of gauze for the veil. Stick it on the queen's head.

7

Castle

Materials

* thick cardboard
* card stock
* 5 toilet tissue tubes
* egg carton
* poster paint
* clay
* felt
* crayons
* sponge
* paintbrush
* toothpick
* marker
* scissors
* white glue

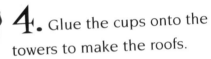

4. Glue the cups onto the towers to make the roofs. Let dry. Mold five small clay cones and glue one onto each roof. Let dry.

3. Cut out five cups from an egg carton. Paint them any color you wish. Let dry. Paint or draw the tiles. Let dry.

2. Paint the tubes any color you wish. Let the paint dry. Use a sponge to add a light layer of poster paint. Let dry. Paint the windows. Let dry.

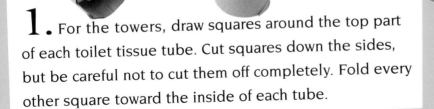

1. For the towers, draw squares around the top part of each toilet tissue tube. Cut squares down the sides, but be careful not to cut them off completely. Fold every other square toward the inside of each tube.

5. For the central tower, cut a rectangle out of cardboard. Cut and paint the cardboard rectangle the same way you did the tubes. Let dry.

6. Fold the rectangle into four equal parts. Glue the edges closed and let dry. Paint the windows. Let dry.

7. Glue one of the round towers onto the side of the rectangular tower so that it does not touch the ground. Let dry.

8. Draw the castle walls on cardboard and cut them out at different lengths. Paint them the same way you painted the towers, but paint both sides of the walls. Let dry. On the shortest piece of wall, cut a door, leaving the bottom attached.

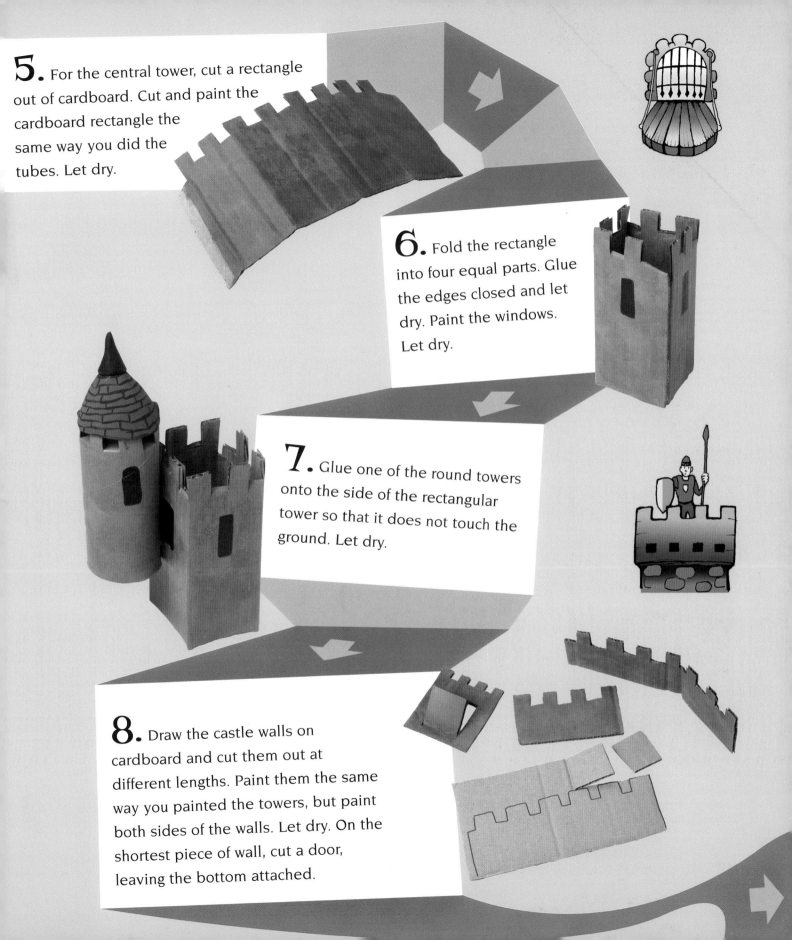

9. Glue the walls to the towers to form the outside of the castle.

10. Cut a piece of card stock a little larger than the castle. Glue a smaller piece of card stock onto the middle of the larger one. Let dry. Decorate the edges with crayons to make the water in the moat. Place the castle on the card stock with the rectangular tower in the middle.

11. For the flag, cut a small rectangle out of felt. Cut a small triangle out of one end of the rectangle. Decorate the flag as you wish. Glue the flag around a toothpick. Let dry. Stick the flag into the clay tip of the central tower.

A big shadow gets
closer to the castle!

Minstrel

Materials

- craft wire
- felt
- clay
- card stock
- marker
- scissors
- white glue
- toothpick

1. Make a human figure out of craft wire.

2. Make the different pieces of clothes with different colors of felt. Make two sets so that they cover the front and back of the body.

3. Glue the two sets of clothing to the wire. Let dry. Bend the figure so that he looks like he is sitting down.

4. Make the head and the hands out of clay. Stick them into the ends of the wire.

6. Draw a mandolin on card stock. Use a marker to draw the strings. Cut out the mandolin and place it in the minstrel's arms.

5. Mold the eyes and a nose from clay. Attach them to the head. Mold the hair out of a flat piece of clay. Use a toothpick to decorate the hair. Attach the hair to the head. Draw a mouth.

I will sing a song about a princess and a dragon!

Princess

The princess listens to the minstrel's song.

Materials

- toilet tissue tube
- marker
- poster paint
- tissue paper
- yarn
- white glue
- paintbrush
- scissors

6. For the hair, tie some yarn together and glue it onto the hat. Let dry. Tie her hair back with another piece of yarn.

1. Draw the princess on a toilet tissue tube. Cut her out.

2. On an extra piece of toilet tissue tube, draw a cone-shaped hat. Cut it out.

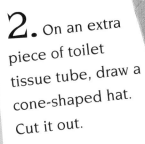

3. Paint the dress and hat any color you wish. Let dry. Paint some details on the dress. Let dry.

Oh, no! The dragon's tail!

4. Paint the princess's head. Let dry. Draw eyes, a nose, and a mouth.

5. Glue a piece of tissue paper to the cone hat to make a veil. Let dry. Glue the hat to her head. Let dry.

Materials

* egg carton
* card stock
* felt
* clay
* poster paint
* marker
* paintbrush
* scissors
* white glue

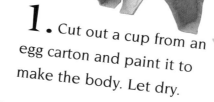

1. Cut out a cup from an egg carton and paint it to make the body. Let dry.

2. Draw a head with a long neck, and a tail on card stock with a marker. Cut them out.

3. Cut a long, thin strip of felt. Cut triangles along one of the edges. Glue it along the top of the body. Let dry. Draw the feet on felt. Cut them out and glue them to the body. Let dry.

4. Cut two more strips of felt with triangles along the edges. Glue them to the dragon's neck and the tail. Let dry.

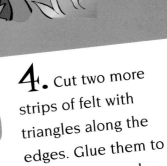

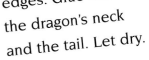

16

Dragon

7. Draw a flame on card stock and cut it out. Draw a smaller flame on card stock and cut it out. Glue the smaller flame on top of the larger flame. Let dry. Glue the flame to the dragon's mouth. Let dry.

The dragon burned the princess's dress!

6. Glue the head and the tail to the body underneath the cup. Let dry.

5. Make clay eyes and glue them to the head. Let dry.

That was my favorite dress!

Catapult

Materials

- corrugated paper
- string
- clay
- toothpick
- cloth
- scissors
- white glue

1. Cut six strips of corrugated paper. Glue them together to make two triangles. Let dry.

2. Cut two more strips of corrugated paper a little longer than the others. Cut a V into one end of each strip. Glue one strip to the middle of each triangle. Let dry.

3. Cut three more strips of corrugated paper. Fold the ends and glue them to the two triangles, joining them together. Let dry.

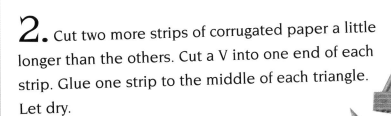

4. To make the lever, cut five more strips of corrugated paper, one longer than the rest. Glue them together as shown in the photo. Let dry. Glue a toothpick behind the lever, just below the triangular end of it. Let dry.

What a powerful catapult!

6. Cut a piece of cloth and tie it at two ends with string. Tie it to the thin end of the lever. Use clay to make balls for the stones. Place a stone inside the cloth.

5. For the catapult's counterweight, roll a piece of corrugated paper and tie it with three pieces of string. Tie it to the triangular end of the lever.

19

1. Draw a horse on cardboard with marker. Draw the cloak that covers it.

Materials

- thick cardboard
- poster paint
- paintbrush
- card stock
- felt
- clay
- marker
- yarn
- white glue
- scissors
- toothpick

2. Use poster paint to decorate the cloak any way you wish. Let dry.

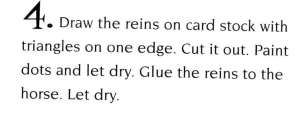

3. Paint the eye and the hooves. Let dry.

4. Draw the reins on card stock with triangles on one edge. Cut it out. Paint dots and let dry. Glue the reins to the horse. Let dry.

Horse

Princess, I dedicate this tournament to you!

6. Use a toothpick to draw blades of grass on a piece of clay. Stick the horse into the grass to make it stand on its own.

5. Cut a rectangle from felt. Glue it over the horse's back like a saddle. Glue some yarn for the tail. Let dry.

The horse is dressed up for the tournament!

The Knight jousts in her honor.

Materials

- clay
- tissue paper
- toothpicks
- white glue
- scissors

Thank you, noble knight.

6. Cut two pieces of tissue paper, each a different color. Glue one on top of the other on the knight's back for the cape.

1. Mix different colors of clay together. Make a thick rectangle out of clay for the body.

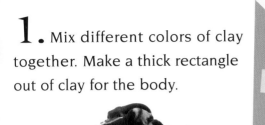

2. Make legs out of two thick, long pieces of clay. Make knee pads out of two small strips of clay and attach them to the legs. Attach the legs to the body with toothpicks.

3. For the arms, drape a long, thin piece of clay across the top of the body. Form a ball of clay for the head. Attach the head to the body with a toothpick.

4. Stick a small clay ball on top of the head. For the visor, add a piece of clay where the mouth should be. Use a toothpick to decorate the armor.

5. For the feather, take a small piece of clay and draw lines on it with a toothpick. Attach the feather to the head with a toothpick.

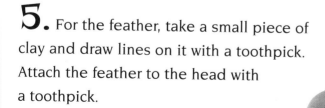

Materials

* dowel
* clay
* poster paint
* card stock
* paintbrush
* white glue
* scissors

Shield and Lance

1. Paint the dowel any color you wish. Let dry.

2. Paint lines in two other colors around the dowel. Let dry. Mold the bottom of the lance from clay.

3. Draw a shield on card stock. Cut it out.

4. Decorate the shield as you wish. Let dry.

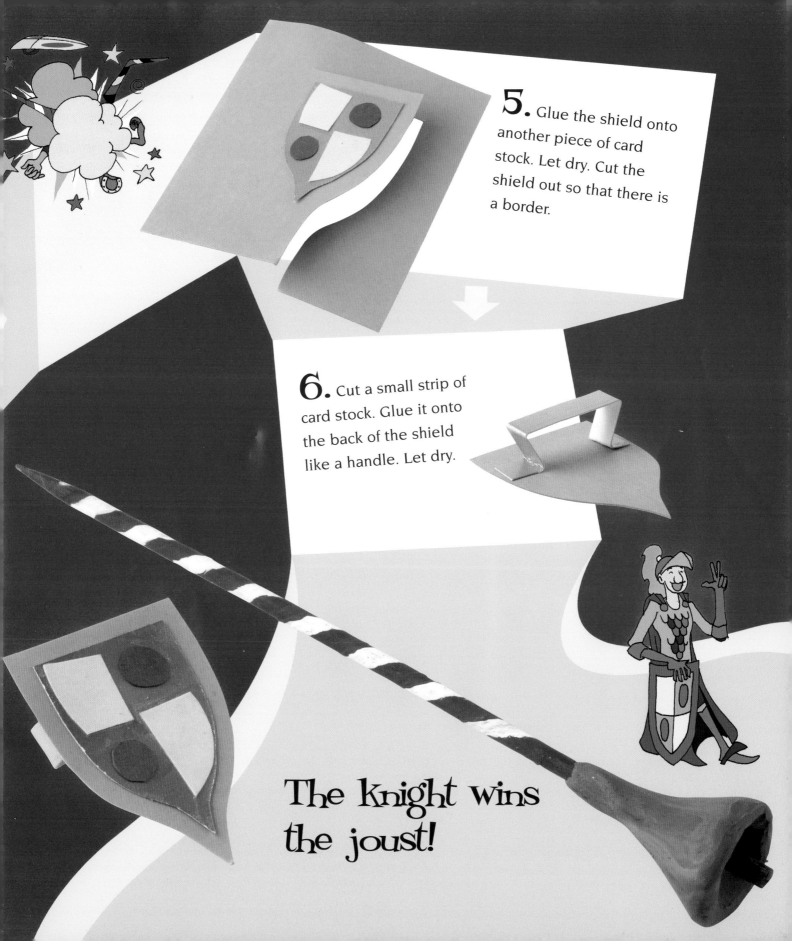

5. Glue the shield onto another piece of card stock. Let dry. Cut the shield out so that there is a border.

6. Cut a small strip of card stock. Glue it onto the back of the shield like a handle. Let dry.

The knight wins the joust!

Court Jester

Materials

- clay
- toothpicks
- plastic knife

The court jester
performs at
the end of the
tournament!

1. Make two arms with clay. Stick a toothpick into one of the arms. Gently bend the clay so that it stands on its own.

2. Make a thick clay rectangle for the body. Pass the toothpick through the body to attach it to the bent arm. Stick the other arm to the front of the body.

3. Mold the legs from a single piece of clay, ending in two pointy shoes. Add two small balls of clay to the tips for decoration. Attach the legs to the body with a toothpick.

4. Use clay to make the head, eyes, and nose. Attach the eyes and nose to the head. Use a toothpick to draw the mouth.

5. Flatten a piece of clay. Cut out a hat with three points with a plastic knife. Add three small balls of clay to the tips for decoration. Place the hat on the head. Attach the head to the body with a toothpick.

Create your own story with all the crafts in this book!

A Medieval Tale
Many years ago . . .

King William ruled in a castle and protected his subjects. Queen Anna, his wife, ruled by the king's side.

The castle door is strong and will keep any enemies out. The royal guards defend the castle.

Princess Lily looks out from the window of the highest tower. A huge shadow appears on the walls.

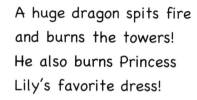

A minstrel sings about a princess who is kidnapped by a beast. His music is heard throughout the castle. As the princess listens, she dreams about her prince.

Suddenly, something startles her . . .

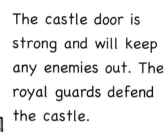

A huge dragon spits fire and burns the towers! He also burns Princess Lily's favorite dress!

Lily is angry. She loads a boulder onto a catapult and hits the dragon.

Victory! In the castle, a tournament is held in honor of the brave princess. Thomas, a knight, heads over to the tournament on his horse.

Thomas dedicates the joust to Princess Lily. She smiles at him.

Thomas and his opponent, James, clash lances and shields.

Thomas defeats James!

I am the court jester! I entertain the kingdom with my silly act!

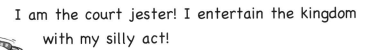

Until our next adventure!

Enslow Elementary, an imprint of Enslow Publishers, Inc.
Enslow Elementary® is a registered trademark of Enslow Publishers, Inc.

English edition copyright © 2011 by Enslow Publishers, Inc.

Translated from the Spanish edition by Stacey Juana Pontoriero.
Edited and produced by Enslow Publishers, Inc.

Library-in-Cataloging Publication Data

Llimós Plomer, Anna.
[Crea tu. Castillo medieval. English]
Medieval castle adventure crafts / Anna Llimós.
p. cm. — (Fun adventure crafts)
Includes bibliographical references and index.
Summary: "Provides step-by-step instructions on how to make eleven simple medieval-themed crafts, such as a knight, castle, dragon, and more, and it includes a story for kids to tell with their crafts"—Provided by publisher.
ISBN 978-0-7660-3734-2
1. Handicraft—Europe—History—To 1500—Juvenile literature. 2. Civilization, Medieval, in art—Juvenile literature. 3. Castles in art—Juvenile literature. I. Title. II. Title: Castillo medieval.
TT55.L5413 2010
745.5—dc22
                            2009041470
ISBN-13 978-0-7660-3735-9 (paperback ed.)

Originally published in Spanish under the title *Crea tu . . . Castillo medieval.*
Copyright © 2008 PARRAMÓN EDICIONES, S.A., - World Rights.
Published by Parramón Ediciones, S.A., Barcelona, Spain.
Text and exercises: Anna Llimós
Illustrator: Àlex Sagarra
Photographs: Nos & Soto

Printed in Spain

122009 Gráficas 94 S.L., Barcelona, Spain

10 9 8 7 6 5 4 3 2 1

Read About

Books

Groves, Marsha. *Medieval Projects You Can Do!* New York: Crabtree Pub. Co., 2006.

Sadler, Judy Ann. *The New Jumbo Book of Easy Crafts.* Toronto: Kids Can Press, 2009.

Internet Addresses

Fairytale Castle Craft
<http://www.activityvillage.co.uk/fairytale_castle_craft.htm>

King Craft, DLTK's Crafts for Kids
<http://www.dltk-kids.com/crafts/mardigras/mking.html>

Index